Bottlenose dolphin, Quest Learning Center, Hawaii

NATIONAL GEOGRAPHIC KIDS

EVERYTHING
DOLPHINS

NATIONAL GEOGRAPHIC

Using teamwork, these long-beaked common dolphins herd sardines into a tight ball, making it a cinch to gobble them by the mouthful.

NATIONAL GEOGRAPHIC KIDS

EVERYTHING DOLPHINS

BY ELIZABETH CARNEY
with National Geographic Explorer Flip Nicklin

NATIONAL GEOGRAPHIC
WASHINGTON, D.C.

CONTENTS

A common dolphin leaps to get a better view of the surrounding waters off Sydney, Australia.

A bottlenose dolphin pod swims through turquoise waters off the coast of Hawaii.

INTRODUCTION

IMAGINE THAT INSTEAD
OF BEING BORN TO LIVE ON LAND, YOU WERE MEANT TO LIVE IN THE SEA.

What would you look like? How would you communicate? What abilities would you have? (Remember: You're a mammal; you still have to breathe air. No cheating with gills!)

If you imagined yourself like a dolphin, you could do well in an underwater world. Dolphins are perfectly suited for undersea life. With their powerful bodies and sleek fins, dolphins can swim up to seven times faster than the fastest swimming human, hold their breath for over ten minutes, and dive up to 2,000 feet (610 m)!

As any scuba diver knows, there's no talking underwater. But this isn't a problem for dolphins. They're masters of underwater communication. You would have to be, in order to keep complex relationships with your family and friends, like dolphins do.

In many ways, dolphins are like underwater versions of ourselves. Maybe that's why many people find them so fascinating. Let's take a deep breath and jump into the dolphins' world!

EXPLORER'S CORNER

Ahoy! I'm Flip Nicklin. I'm an underwater photographer. I've been slipping beneath the waves to take pictures of whales and dolphins for most of my life. Over the course of more than 5,500 dives, I've had some wild encounters with dolphins. The times they've let me into their world have been the most memorable moments of my life. When you see me, I'll fill you in on the secrets of these masters of the sea.

1
MEET THE DOLPHIN

A bottlenose dolphin makes a splash while peeking its head out of the water in Hawaii.

An Amazon river dolphin adds a splash of pink to the Rio Negro in Brazil.

WHAT IS A DOLPHIN?

DOLPHIN

* Tails move up and down.
* Warm-blooded
* Lungs

DOLPHINS HAVE FINS AND SPEND THEIR WHOLE LIVES UNDERWATER, but their similarities with fish end there. As mammals like us, dolphins nurse their young with milk. They're warm-blooded and have a fixed body temperature. Because they have lungs, dolphins must surface periodically to take in air through a hole on top of their body. They're even born with a tiny patch of hair on their chin!

FISH, ON THE OTHER HAND, TAKE OXYGEN OUT OF THE WATER THROUGH GILLS.

They have scales instead of skin and hair, and they lay eggs. A fish's body temperature changes with the temperature of the water that it's in.

Dolphins and fish even swim differently. Dolphins flex their tails up and down to zoom through the water. Fish bend their tails from side to side.

Dolphins' underwater moves may seem astonishing—just don't call them fishy!

FISH

* Tails move side to side.
* Cold-blooded
* Gills

FIN FACT LIKE US, A DOLPHIN GETS ONE SET OF TEETH TO LAST A LIFETIME.

DOLPHIN FAMILY TREE

DOLPHIN AND WHALE LAND ANCESTORS

BALEEN WHALES

TOOTHED WHALES

CETACEAN FAMILY

PORPOISES

DOLPHINS

RIVER DOLPHINS

OCEAN BOUND

Whales and dolphins are the distant relatives of hoofed animals such as deer, hippos, and bison. How is this possible? Well, about 50 million years ago, whales and dolphins began evolving from meat-eating land mammals that began moving to the oceans in search of food.

MILLIONS OF YEARS AGO, DOLPHINS' ANCESTORS

HAD LEGS AND WALKED ON LAND! All cetaceans—the group that includes dolphins, whales, and porpoises—are likely descended from a group of meat-eating, hoofed mammals. This ancestor began moving into the sea around 50 million years ago, probably because food was abundant there.

Over the years, the cetacean family tree branched out from those early ancestors into the three main groups that we see today—dolphins, whales, and porpoises. But you can find evidence of modern cetaceans' land-loving origins. Their skeletons contain small, rod-shaped bones near their pelvis. These bones are the remains of hind legs—evolutionary leftovers after millions of years of turning into full-time swimmers.

WHALES

FIN FACT A BLUE WHALE'S HEART IS AS BIG AS A SMALL CAR.

WHALES, DOLPHINS, PORPOISES: WHAT'S THE DIFFERENCE?

There are more than 80 different types of cetaceans and sometimes the distinctions between them are a bit confusing. For example, all dolphins are whales (toothed whales, to be specific), but not all whales are dolphins. Whales come in another variety called baleen whales, which are very different from dolphins. Instead of teeth, these animals have comb-like plates that filter huge quantities of food from the water. Baleen whales are the giants of the sea, and include humpback whales, bowhead whales, and blue whales— the largest animals ever!

Porpoises are like dolphins' cousins. Porpoises are almost always smaller than dolphins and have smaller, rounded snouts. Dolphins usually have larger foreheads. What's the easiest way to tell dolphins and porpoises apart? Ask them to smile! Dolphins have pointy, cone-shaped teeth. Porpoises have more rounded chompers.

DOLPHIN

PORPOISE

WHERE TO FIND DOLPHINS

DOLPHINS CAN BE FOUND IN EVERY OCEAN IN THE WORLD

—and even some rivers. Most dolphins live in the warm waters around the Equator. But some species prefer chilly waters. Scientists consider all dolphins to be toothed whales. That explains why some dolphins have "whale" in their names. If you're cruising over the open ocean, chances are that you're passing through a dolphin's habitat!

EXPLORER'S CORNER

Photographing dolphins has taken me all over the world, from the crystal blue waters of the Bahamas to the frigid coast of Argentina. I've even had pink Amazon river dolphins nibble at my heels while at a lake in Brazil. When I'm underwater with dolphins, I have to be aware that I'm a visitor to their world. I never chase them or interfere with their behavior. I try to be a respectful observer. Sometimes dolphins get curious about me, though. They'll often swim up to the camera to check me out. Sometimes they'll even try to play with me! Maybe they're showing me what awkward swimmers we humans can be.

ASIA

PACIFIC OCEAN

AUSTRALIA

PACIFIC OCEAN

Orcas are found in oceans all over the world. These jumbo-size dolphins usually stay in the same place year-round, but they'll go on the move if they can't find enough food.

False killer whales are found all over the warm waters of the Atlantic, Pacific, and Indian Oceans. Unlike some other species, these dolphins prefer deep waters.

The little **Hector's dolphin** can be found in the coastal waters off New Zealand. They usually stick close to the shoreline but have been known to venture into deeper waters on occasion.

Map Key
- Polar waters
- Temperate waters
- Tropical and subtropical waters

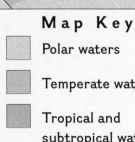

ARCTIC OCEAN

NORTH AMERICA

EUROPE

You'll find the smart and social **Atlantic spotted dolphin** in the warm, tropical waters of the Atlantic Ocean. These dolphins spend most of their time over sand flats in shallow waters.

ATLANTIC OCEAN

AFRICA

SOUTH AMERICA

The **Amazon river dolphin** can be found in the Amazon and Orinoco Rivers in South America. They have also been spotted in lakes, small channels—even in rapids and below waterfalls!

The **Irrawaddy dolphin** likes to swim along the coasts of countries all over Southeast Asia, including India, Thailand, Cambodia, and Bangladesh. These dolphins prefer muddy waters at the mouths of rivers.

The **Dusky dolphin** lives near the cool coasts of South America, South Africa, southern Australia, and New Zealand. Every morning, these expert swimmers move to deeper waters in search of food.

The southwest Atlantic Ocean is where you will find the unique **Commerson's dolphin**. These creatures prefer shallow waters along the coasts and use the tides to help them swim toward the shore.

INDIAN OCEAN

Found in the Indian and Pacific Oceans, the **Indo-Pacific humpback dolphin** prefers warm, tropical waters and likes to swim close to shore. It has been spotted in bays, coral reefs, and mangrove forests, too.

FIN FACT FOLLOWING A FLOOD, AMAZON RIVER DOLPHINS CAN SWIM THROUGH PARTS OF FORESTS.

ANTARCTICA

ECHOLOCATION

Dolphins have a special superpower that makes their underwater ways easier. They use a type of sonar called echolocation to hunt and navigate.

Let's say some delicious fish and shellfish are buried in the sand. Dolphins send a stream of clicks to the seafloor.

The way the sound bounces back gives the dolphins a picture of what's ahead of them.

They know exactly where to dig up a tasty meal. It's kind of like having x-ray vision, but instead of sight dolphins rely on sound and hearing.

Atlantic Spotted Dolphins

WATER WONDERS

STROKE BY STROKE

Commerson's Dolphin

A dolphin swims forward by moving its fluke, or tail fin, up and down. Its body ripples like a wave. When a dolphin moves its tail up, the middle of its body dips down. When its tail moves down, the dolphin's midsection arches up.

DOLPHINS HAVE MANY

ADAPTATIONS THAT MAKE THEM SUITED FOR SEA LIFE.

Their smooth, hairless bodies glide through water with ease. Dolphins stay warm in cold water with the help of layers of fat under their skin called blubber. A blowhole at the top of their head allows for easy breathing at the water's surface.

You might be wondering: How do dolphins ever sleep when they have to return to the surface to breathe so frequently? Dolphins sleep with only half their brain at a time! The other half stays active so dolphins can surface to breathe. One eye even keeps a lookout for dolphins' top natural enemy—sharks.

DOLPHINS "SLEEP" FOR ABOUT EIGHT HOURS A DAY, ALTHOUGH THEY ARE NEVER FULLY UNCONSCIOUS.

Bottlenose Dolphin

FIN FACT SOMETIMES DOLPHINS "SURF" ON BOATS' BOW WAVES. THIS GIVES THEM A BOOST OF SPEED.

A PHOTOGRAPHIC DIAGRAM

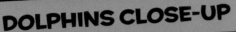

DOLPHINS CLOSE-UP

DORSAL FIN A dorsal fin helps dolphins stay balanced in the water. The height of the fin can vary widely. An orca's dorsal fin can be six feet (1.8 m) tall! Some species barely have one at all. Their fin looks more like a hump.

DOLPHINS ARE DESIGNED

FOR A FULLY AQUATIC LIFE. As sea predators, dolphins also have top-notch hunting skills. Here are some of the features that give dolphins their underwater abilities.

FLUKE A powerful tail fin called a fluke propels dolphins through the water.

SKIN A dolphin's smooth skin feels like rubber. Like our skin, a dolphin's is delicate and sensitive to the touch. It's kept smooth by constantly being rubbed off and replaced.

FIN FACT A BOTTLENOSE DOLPHIN REPLACES ITS OUTERMOST LAYER OF SKIN EVERY TWO HOURS.

BLOWHOLE Dolphins breathe through a hole near the back of their head called a blowhole. Dolphins exhale and inhale extremely fast, taking a breath in a third of a second. Air blasts from the blowhole at 100 miles an hour (160 kmh).

MELON This fatty, rounded section of a dolphin's forehead is called a melon. It's used to focus and transmit the sound waves produced for echolocation.

ROSTRUM A dolphin's beak-like snout is called a rostrum.

EARS A dolphin's ear holes are easy to miss. They're about the size of a crayon tip. Yet dolphins have some of the best hearing in the animal kingdom.

TEETH Dolphins swallow food whole, but they still have up to 250 pointy, cone-shaped teeth for grabbing fish.

FLIPPERS are dolphins' steering mechanism, helping them start, stop, and turn.

EYES A dolphin's eyeballs move independently of each other. For example, one eye can look straight ahead, while the other looks straight up. Try it! Not so easy, right?

Pacific White-Sided Dolphin

2 LIFE OF A DOLPHIN

Bottlenose dolphins leap in the air as the sun sets. Dolphins leap for all sorts of reasons: to scope out schools of fish, to communicate, to get their bearings, and sometimes just for fun!

BABY'S FIRST STROKES

FROM THE MOMENT IT'S
BORN, A BABY DOLPHIN CAN SWIM.

Its mother gently nudges the baby to surface, where it gasps its first breath of air. Dolphins have to be born on the move. It's the only way to escape sharks, their top predator. For an extra protection boost, mother dolphins often band together in small "nursery groups." These groups let the youngsters play while the grown-ups look out for danger.

Young dolphins nurse on their mothers' milk for their first year of life. They'll stay with their mothers for three to six years, learning how to catch their own food and socializing with other dolphins.

TAIL-LY HO!
Dolphin babies are usually born tail first. Sometimes another dolphin from the pod, called an "auntie," helps with the birth.

Bottlenose Dolphin

EXPLORER'S CORNER

Mother dolphins have much to teach their young about how to survive in the vast ocean. Fortunately, they are patient teachers. I once saw a mother orca in Alaska teaching her baby how to catch fish. The mother chased a salmon, keeping it close, while her youngster tried to grab it. More than a game of tag, this lesson will help the baby survive on its own one day.

Orca

Hawaiian Spinner

GOT MILK?
Baby dolphins nurse as often as four times an hour for about five to ten seconds per feeding. They completely depend on mom's milk until they learn how to hunt fish.

Newborns follow mom's every move and never leave her side.

FIN FACT AT BIRTH, A BABY DOLPHIN'S FINS ARE SOFT AND FLOPPY. THE FINS GRADUALLY BECOME FIRM.

A pod of Commerson's dolphins patrols the waters off the tip of South America.

HOME IS WHERE MY POD IS

IT'S A BIG OCEAN OUT THERE.
TO INCREASE THEIR CHANCE OF SURVIVAL (AND FOR SOME COMPANY), DOLPHINS STICK TOGETHER IN GROUPS CALLED PODS. These groups vary in size from 2 to more than 15 individuals. Pod members form complex relationships with one another. They'll also share survival duties. Some look out for danger. Others help take care of the young. There's time for fun and games as well, and dolphins, like humans, often have their preferred playmates.

Although dolphins might look as if they're always getting along, don't be fooled. Dolphins can be aggressive. In fights over females or who will lead the pod, males can deliver "kicks" with their powerful flukes, snap their jaws, and even bite.

Researchers are just beginning to understand how important dolphins' relationships are to their survival. New findings show that female dolphins have more success raising calves if they have relationships with other successful mothers. Maybe that's where they get the best parenting advice!

ALTHOUGH MANY DOLPHINS LIVE IN PODS, SOME, LIKE THE AMAZON RIVER DOLPHIN, LIVE ALONE.

Bottlenose Dolphins

FIN FACT SOMETIMES, SEVERAL DOLPHIN PODS JOIN TOGETHER TO BRIEFLY FORM A "SUPERPOD," A HERD OF UP TO A THOUSAND DOLPHINS.

HOW TO SPEAK DOLPHIN

WHEN RESEARCHERS LISTEN IN ON DOLPHINS IN THE WILD, THEY OFTEN HEAR A LOT OF CHATTER. Dolphins use a distinct set of sounds to communicate: chirps, whistles, squeaks, clicks, and a series of clicks, called click trains.

Different combinations of sounds seem to mean different things in different situations. Dolphins even have signature whistles for themselves that function like their names! Each dolphin chooses its own signature whistle, usually by its first birthday. The "name" sticks for at least ten more years.

You don't have to speak dolphin to know that this group of bottlenose dolphins is having fun. In a favorite game, dolphins blow bubbles or rings of air and then dive through them.

WHISTLE

CHIRP

CLICK

FIN FACT DOLPHINS CAN MAKE SOUND UNDERWATER WITHOUT MOVING THEIR MOUTHS.

Two dolphins communicate by going bottlenose to bottlenose.

Spotted Dolphins

BODY LANGUAGE

When people raise their hand to give a high five, open their arms for a hug, or angrily cross their arms, you likely know what they're communicating. In the same way, dolphins also use gesture, touch, and body posture to get their point across. Oftentimes, the meaning of a dolphin's touch or posture depends on the situation. It's like how a waving hand can mean hello or goodbye.

FISHING EXPERTS

Dusky Dolphins

DOLPHINS ARE CARNIVORES.
THEY SURVIVE OFF THE FLESH OF OTHER ANIMALS—
MAINLY FISH. Because of their large size and active lifestyle, dolphins have to catch an average of 20 to 50 pounds (9 to 23 kg) of food a day. Fortunately, catching fish is a cinch when you're a dolphin!

FIN FACT TO GET TO FISH IN A HURRY, SOME DOLPHINS TAKE LONG, FLAT LEAPS IN THE AIR. BECAUSE AIR IS NOT AS DENSE AS WATER, THEY TRAVEL FASTER.

Dolphins and tuna share a meal as they feed on a school of small fish near the Costa Rican coast.

ON THE MENU

As you can imagine, seafood makes up the vast majority of most dolphins' diets. But each type of dolphin's preferred menu can vary widely. The type of prey that's available in a species' habitat determines its diet.

BOTTLENOSE DOLPHIN

Equally at home in the Atlantic and Pacific Oceans, bottlenoses enjoy small schooling fish like mackerel and mullet. They'll also happily dig in on shrimp, eel, and crab.

WHITE-SIDED DOLPHIN

This Pacific Ocean species snacks on salmon, pollock, anchovies, squid, and herring.

HECTOR'S DOLPHIN

This small species likes trolling the seafloor for its meals, picking up flounder, red cod, and crab.

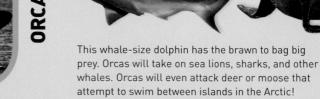

ORCA

This whale-size dolphin has the brawn to bag big prey. Orcas will take on sea lions, sharks, and other whales. Orcas will even attack deer or moose that attempt to swim between islands in the Arctic!

Dolphins often snag their meals in groups, and many types of dolphins have their own hunting strategies. Duskies leap high to scan the horizon for feasting seabirds. The birds pinpoint the location of a meal. Spotted dolphins herd fish into a tight group called a "bait ball" so they're easier to grab. A group of bottlenose dolphins in Florida has been observed wrangling fish within rings of mud they've kicked up with their flukes. There's no end to what dolphins will think of next!

A PHOTO GALLERY

DOLPHINS EVERYWHERE!

A Peale's dolphin hitches a ride on the wave created by a boat's bow.

An Indo-Pacific humpback dolphin gives a toothy grin.

Above or below the waves, dolphins are real show-offs!

DOLPHINS ARE A BIG FAMILY OF ANIMALS that have many shapes, sizes, and colors. No matter where they're from or what form they take, dolphins have a knack for making life in the sea look fun!

Tiny and rare Hector's dolphins cruise in a pod off the coast of New Zealand.

A bottlenose and Risso's dolphin form an aquatic alliance.

It's easy to see why the Latin name for this short-finned pilot whale means "globe head."

Racing Clymene dolphins rocket from the water in the Gulf of Mexico.

Is that a shark? Fear not—the curved shape tells you this is a friendly fin!

An hourglass dolphin breaches the frigid Antarctic waters.

A pantropical spotted dolphin catches air during a surf session.

3

A BIG, BLUE WORLD

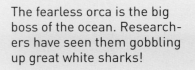

The fearless orca is the big boss of the ocean. Researchers have seen them gobbling up great white sharks!

DOLPHINS IN DISGUISE

NOT ALL

DOLPHINS LOOK ALIKE. In fact some species look downright weird! There are more than 40 species of dolphins that live all over the world, but you'd never guess that some of these swift swimmers are related. One has a super-long beak, while its cousin has no beak at all, and another is covered in scars from frequent fighting. But no matter how they look, they're all part of one big, finned family. Now let's meet some of the dolphin family's oddball relatives!

ORCA
Don't let its titanic size or "killer whale" nickname fool you: This school bus-size sea predator is a dolphin.

IRRAWADDY DOLPHIN
These dolphins, found in both coastal waters and some freshwater rivers, are experts at catching dinner. They spit streams of water to confuse fish, making them a cinch to snatch.

PYGMY KILLER WHALE
One of several dolphin species with the word "whale" in its name, the pygmy killer whale resembles its much larger cousin, the orca.

HECTOR'S DOLPHIN
The smallest dolphin, this 4-foot-long (1.2 m) species is shorter than an orca's dorsal fin. It's also one of the rarest dolphins.

RIGHT WHALE DOLPHIN

See anything missing on these dolphins? Right whale dolphins are the only members of the dolphin family that lack dorsal fins. Social seafarers, they've been spotted in pods of nearly 3,000 individuals.

RISSO'S DOLPHIN

Born with dark skin that turns gray as they age, these large dolphins look like the old men of the sea. Fights with other dolphins leave the Risso's body battered with scars.

HOURGLASS DOLPHIN

Sailors called these small, cold-water mammals "skunk dolphins," but not because they smell bad. The dolphin's white markings look like a skunk's stripe.

AMAZON RIVER DOLPHIN

This largest of the river dolphins will have you seeing pink. The scrappy adult males develop pinkish scar tissue that flushes crimson when they exert themselves.

FIN FACT DOLPHINS HAVE TWO STOMACHS! ONE IS USED TO STORE FOOD, AND THE OTHER IS USED TO DIGEST IT.

DOLPHIN QUEST

HUMANS CAN ONLY BE VISITORS

TO THE DOLPHINS' WORLD. Unlike scientists such as Jane Goodall, who moved into a Tanzanian forest to study chimps, dolphin experts can only get brief glimpses of their subjects before it's time to return to land. Sometimes, it's difficult to even find dolphins in their vast habitats. But fortunately, dolphins sometimes come to us. Many species of dolphins like to surf the waves at the bow of speeding boats. Or help fishermen herd fish into nets. Or make spectacular leaps into the air when boats are around. Maybe they're just showing off. Or perhaps dolphins are as curious about us as we are about them.

EXPLORER'S CORNER

Although swimming with dolphins looks like fun, it's important to remember that dolphins are like any wild animal. They can be unpredictable and sometimes aggressive. In the United States it's illegal to chase, harm, or interact with any marine mammal in the wild. That includes dolphins. Programs for swimming with tame dolphins exist in some areas. But there are other ways to see dolphins without getting your feet wet. You can observe dolphins at some aquariums. You could also spy on dolphins in the wild on whale-watching tours. When I photograph dolphins, I always have a permit and make sure to keep my distance so that the animals are not disturbed.

A girl shows off a smile as she swims with a tame bottlenose dolphin in Hawaii.

DRESSED FOR STUDYING DOLPHINS

MASK Allows you to keep your eyes open underwater by keeping salt water out

SNORKEL Plastic tube fitted with a mouthpiece at one end that lets you breathe while swimming just below the surface

BATHING SUIT (A wet suit in cold waters)

UNDERWATER CAMERA AND SOUND RECORDER Scientists studying dolphin behavior often must record dolphins' interactions with waterproof equipment.

FINS Since human feet have little surface area for moving water, we swim much slower than dolphins. Long, flat rubber fins help even things up.

FIN FACT BOTTLENOSE DOLPHINS CAN LIVE MORE THAN 40 YEARS. ORCAS CAN LIVE TO BE 90!

HIDDEN DANGERS

Tourists rescued this baby dolphin after it became trapped in a fishing net. The tiny mammal bears the scars of its struggle.

UP UNTIL 20 YEARS AGO,
RUN-INS WITH HUMANS WERE DOLPHINS'
main cause of death. Dolphins were scooped up in droves as accidental catch in tuna fishermen's nets. Almost two-thirds of the dolphins in eastern tropical Pacific waters were killed this way. In this region, dolphins and tuna often swim together. Since surfacing dolphins are easy to spot, fishermen used dolphins as a marker for tuna.

In the early 1990s, the United States passed laws that called for "dolphin-safe" ways of harvesting tuna. Fishermen could no longer use dolphins as an easy way to target their catch. They also had to use nets that dolphins could escape from more easily. The result: The amount of fishing-related dolphin deaths plunged. Over time, dolphin populations recovered. Now many countries are committed to dolphin-safe tuna fishing.

FIN FACT SOME DOLPHINS HAVE MORE TEETH THAN CROCODILES.

TUNA
The U.S. has laws that call for "dolphin-safe" ways of harvesting tuna.

OIL BURN
This controlled oil burn helped to prevent oil from spreading after a spill in the Gulf of Mexico.

TODAY, POLLUTION IS THE BIGGEST THREAT TO DOLPHINS. Toxins from oil and gas drilling and chemical run-off from coastlines make dolphins vulnerable to disease and infections. In the year following the massive 2010 oil spill in the Gulf of Mexico, more than 12 times as many bottlenose dolphin bodies washed ashore than usual. It was a chilling reminder that keeping the ocean clean is the only way to keep it safe for dolphins.

AQUARIUM LIFE

IN AQUARIUMS, DOLPHINS OFTEN DAZZLE

ONLOOKERS BY DOING FUNNY STUNTS AND AMAZING ACROBATICS ON CUE. With a hand signal or whistle, dolphin trainers can instruct dolphins to leap through hoops, tail walk, or make spinning jumps. These encounters allow aquarium visitors to witness dolphins' intelligence and athletic ability from the safety of a "splash zone."

For dolphins and their trainers, these shows are just part of the job. Trainers must also teach dolphins behaviors that allow staff to monitor their health and safety. Signals like rolling over for a physical exam or opening their mouths wide for a dental check-up make dolphin care much easier.

Trainers say that dolphins enjoy the mental workout that comes with learning new behaviors. We can't give dolphins an IQ test. But scientists believe that they're at least as crafty as other super-smart species like chimpanzees and elephants. Daily training sessions help captive dolphins use the creative smarts that would be put to test daily in the wild.

HOW TO BE A DOLPHIN TRAINER

Trainers use a technique called positive reinforcement to train dolphins. In positive reinforcement, trainers reward an animal when it performs a desired behavior. For a dolphin, the most common reward is food. A tasty fish functions just like a dog biscuit. A soothing touch, squirts of water, and toys can also be rewards for good dolphin behavior. When the dolphin does the move asked of it, trainers reward it immediately.

There's never a dull—or dry—moment for aquarium visitors who take in a splashy dolphin show.

DOLPHIN DEBATE

NOT EVERYONE AGREES WITH dolphins' presence in aquariums. Since dolphins' natural environment can never be truly replicated in a tank, some scientists and conservationists argue that dolphins shouldn't be kept in captivity at all. They say that dolphins don't get enough exercise or social interaction with their own kind in an aquarium. What do you think?

FIN FACT ABOUT 1,800 DOLPHINS LIVE IN CAPTIVITY WORLDWIDE.

DOLPHIN COMPARISONS

DOLPHINS AND YOU

THINK YOU
COULDN'T BE ANY MORE DIFFERENT
from a water-dwelling whale? You might have more in common with dolphins than you realize.

One dolphin uses a waterproof iPad in training. You might have a few gadgets of your own.

THE iPAD IS THE LATEST HI-TECH TOOL RESEARCHERS ARE USING TO HELP ENHANCE COMMUNICATION BETWEEN HUMANS AND DOLPHINS!

SEAFOOD DELIGHT

Bottlenose Dolphin

Seafood-loving dolphins swallow their catch whole. You might enjoy fresh fish, shrimp, or crab (but cut into bite-size bits).

NAME-CALLING

Bottlenose Dolphins

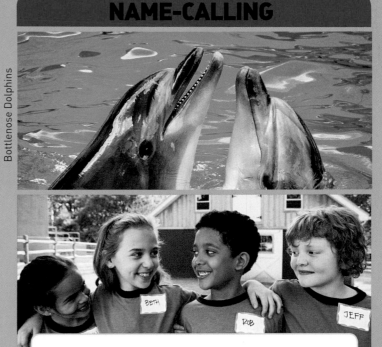

Just as you have a name that you are called, a dolphin has a signature whistle that it goes by.

FAMILY TIES

Bottlenose Dolphins

Dolphins stick with family and friends. You've got your own pod of loved ones.

PLAYTIME ANYTIME

Amazon River Dolphin

Dolphins turn many everyday objects into toys. You do, too, but your play often involves strategy, a set of rules, and your imagination.

FUN
WITH
DOLPHINS

Smart and curious, dolphins have a ball wherever they go. This bottlenose in Germany shares its pool with playful seals.

DOLPHINS IN CULTURE

DOLPHINS HAVE CAPTURED

HUMANS' ATTENTION AND ADMIRATION for thousands of years. When the ancient Greeks spotted dolphins swimming in a ship's wake, they considered it a sign that a smooth voyage was ahead. Many Native American tribes of the Pacific Northwest feature orcas in their traditions, art, and religion. The legends of the Haida people, for example, describe orcas as powerful underwater beings that live in a society much like ours.

Today, humans turn to dolphins as a source of entertainment, study, and companionship. In television shows such as *Flipper* and movies like *Free Willy*, dolphins steal the show. Many aquariums and animal parks have dolphin performances that showcase the animals' physical and mental abilities. Researchers across the world often film and study dolphins to learn about their intelligence and social relationships. Some branches of the U.S. military even use dolphins for jobs like finding underwater explosives! Nice work, Major Dolphin.

FINNED FORCE
Wearing a tracking device on its pectoral fin, a bottlenose dolphin reports for duty in the Arabian Gulf.

An orca carved by Native Americans

Willy leaps to freedom in this scene from the film *Free Willy*.

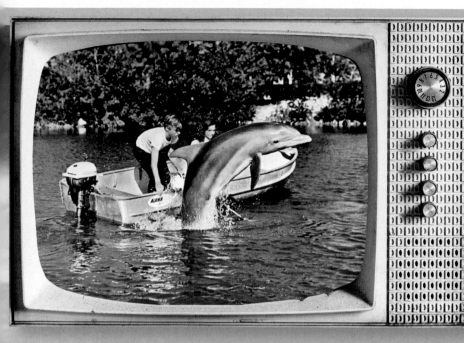

The 1960s TV show *Flipper* turned dolphins into stars.

A pod of dolphins accompanies a Greek god at sea.

Ancient Greeks painted dolphin murals in their palaces.

DOLPHIN IN THE SKY

Ancient stargazers believed a small constellation—or patch of stars—in the northern sky looked like a dolphin. They named it "Delphinus," the Latin word for "dolphin." The constellations Equuleus, a baby horse, and Vulpecula, a fox, border the starry sea creature.

The constellation Delphinus

DOLPHIN MOBILE

You can make dolphin art too! Here's how to make a cool and colorful dolphin mobile.

Materials:
- Two craft sticks or twigs, each at least 12 inches (30 cm) long
- Colored masking or duct tape

- Paper
- Printer (if printing out stencils or templates from the Internet)
- Pencil
- Crayons or markers
- Scissors
- Stapler
- Small cotton balls
- String or ribbon

1 Form a crisscross shape with the two sticks and secure the cross in the middle with the colored masking tape. Set aside.

2 Print out stencils or templates of four of your favorite dolphins or whales from the Internet. Or purchase stencils from a craft store.

3 Draw each dolphin or whale on a piece of paper twice: one facing left, and the other facing right.

4 Color in the animals and carefully cut them out.

5 Match up each dolphin or whale's mirror image and staple the two pieces together along the bottom to form a pocket. Stuff the cotton balls into each pocket. Then staple along the top to close the figures.

6 Staple string or ribbon to the top center of each whale or dolphin. The first string should be about 12 inches (30 cm) long. You can vary the lengths of the three remaining strings so that each animal hangs at a different height.

7 Tie each dolphin or whale around a stick and secure with a small piece of tape.

8 Tie a piece of string to the mobile's center and use it to hang your mobile.

PLAY LIKE A DOLPHIN

Bottlenose Dolphin

A DOLPHIN'S DAY ALWAYS INCLUDES

SOME TIME SPENT CLOWNING AROUND. Dolphins can turn almost any floating object into a toy. Some dolphins drape themselves in seaweed; others toss it into the air and try to catch it. Amazon river dolphins play catch with coconuts. Male dolphins sometimes carry objects when trying to woo females. A male will pick up a branch, a rock, or a clump of weeds and twirl in a circle in an attempt to impress the ladies!

Sometimes dolphins use objects as tools, not just as toys. Some bottlenose dolphins off the coast of Australia cover their noses with sponges as they dig in the ocean floor for food. The sponges serve as protective gloves for their snouts. Dolphins have also been observed pushing massive shells to the water's surface. Then they give the shells a shake to force out fish hiding inside.

Dolphins don't necessarily need props for fun. They can chase one another in a game like tag, jump acrobatically, and cuddle with a playmate. Dolphins even get a kick out of playing with other species. They tease eels to coax them out of their holes and prod puffer fish to make them inflate. Play nice, dolphins!

DOLPHINS' COOL MOVES

Sure, they're great swimmers, but check out the other abilities that make dolphins **ALL-STAR AQUA ATHLETES.**

VERTICAL LEAP
An orca can jump so high that its snout is 40 feet (12 m) out of the water.

SPIN CYCLE
Spinner dolphins rotate in the air—like a football—as they leap.

TAIL WALKING
In this stunt, a dolphin stands on its fluke and scoots across the water. It's a common trick dolphins perform in captivity.

BENDY BODY
Amazon river dolphins have very flexible necks that they use to snake their way through tangled underwater branches.

MY FINNED FRIEND

MAJA KAZAZIC HAD BECOME

used to living with pain—and feeling different. As a teen, Maja lost her leg after she was badly injured during the Bosnian civil war. But even after treatment, an uncomfortable prosthesis—or artificial body part—made every movement painful.

Maja's life changed when she met Winter, a dolphin at Clearwater Marine Aquarium. Winter had lost her tail in a crab trap as a baby. Maja felt a connection with the tailless dolphin.

When Winter got a high-tech tail to help her swim, Maja wondered if a similar product could help her be pain free. The aquarium put Maja in touch with the company that made Winter's prosthesis. Maja received a new leg out of the same advanced materials that helped Winter. Soon the pair were swimming together—one with a new leg, the other with a new tail.

Winter and her new tail became famous and inspired thousands through books, articles, and even a movie. But Winter's biggest fan is still Maja: "She changed my life."

The ocean is a dolphin's toy box. Seaweed, bubbles, a wriggling octopus—all make perfect playthings!

FIN FACT DOLPHINS HAVE LITTLE TO NO SENSE OF SMELL.

WHAT'S YOUR DOLPHIN PERSONALITY?

HAVE YOU EVER
WONDERED WHAT TYPE OF DOLPHIN
you would be? Take this quiz to find out!

1 What type of meal sounds the most delicious to you?
a. A big, meaty meal
b. Sushi-style fish dinner
c. Shellfish and even an occasional turtle
d. Squid, tentacles and all

2 Which statement best describes your approach to social interactions?
a. I'm really close to my mom and always take her advice.
b. My friends and I like to go to big parties.
c. I keep close to my dad and my family.
d. I mainly stick to smaller groups of my closest buddies.

3 Where is your perfect living spot?
a. I like it cold.
b. I'm not picky.
c. I like warm rivers in jungles.
d. I stick to warm spots in the Atlantic Ocean.

4 What color do you like to wear best?
a. Black and white
b. Gray
c. Pink
d. Spots

5 What describes your approach to physical fitness?
a. I focus on strength and power.
b. I need speed and agility.
c. I'm proud of my flexibility.
d. I like to jump and surf.

FIN FACT DOLPHINS DON'T DRINK SEAWATER. THEY GET THE WATER THEY NEED FROM THEIR DIET.

WHAT'S YOUR PLACE IN THE DOLPHIN FAMILY?

IF YOU SCORED MOSTLY A's: You're like the mighty **orca**. You can use your strength and intelligence to survive in frosty places.

IF YOU SCORED MOSTLY B's: You're like the **bottle-nose dolphin**. Your versatility allows you to make it almost anywhere.

IF YOU SCORED MOSTLY C's: You're like the curious **Amazon river dolphin**. Your surprising appearance and unlikely habitat make you fun to know.

IF YOU SCORED MOSTLY D's: You're like the **Atlantic spotted dolphin**. Your fun-loving nature makes you a blast to watch.

SPOT THE DOLPHIN

EVEN LAND-LOVERS
HAVE A FASCINATION with dolphins. They're a big part of our popular culture. If you pay attention, you might spot dolphins everywhere. Can you find the dolphin in each of these photographs?

Wish you were here!

FIN FACT THE DOLPHIN IS THE MASCOT OF MANY SPORTS TEAMS, INCLUDING THE NATIONAL FOOTBALL LEAGUE'S MIAMI DOLPHINS.

PHOTO FINISH

I HAVE BEEN AN UNDERWATER **PHOTOGRAPHER FOR MANY YEARS.** It's a great job because I get to swim with many different kinds of dolphins. But getting the perfect shot of these cool creatures is no easy task. The hardest thing about it is having patience and keeping up with them. Dolphins can swim very fast, so sometimes it's hard to get a picture. Fortunately, there are times when they swim slowly and let us watch them while they interact with one another. On the day I took this picture, I traveled with a team of researchers who study dolphins' habitats and behaviors so that we can better understand dolphins and learn how to protect them.

When I photograph dolphins, there is a lot I have to do to prepare and to make sure I get a great picture. First, I put on a mask, flippers, and a snorkel to help me swim. I also have to protect my camera. I put it in a special case that allows me to take it underwater without damaging it. When I'm close to dolphins, I make sure to stay out of their way, but sometimes the dolphins come close to me on their own.

I took this picture during a trip to the Bahamas, and it was great to be able to get such a wonderful shot of dolphins. During this same trip I had another cool dolphin encounter. One day a group of Atlantic spotted dolphins approached my boat. I was very excited to see them, so I put on my gear and hopped out of the boat and into the water. One of the spotted dolphins came up to me, looked me in the eye, and then swam around me again and again. He was playing a game! I got dizzy from all the spinning and had to stop, so this dolphin decided to go play with someone else. That day I learned that dolphins are good at finding ways to have fun!

Dolphin researcher Dr. Denise Herzing films two spotted dolphins as they swim gracefully in shallow waters 40 miles (60 km) off the coast of the Bahamas.

AFTERWORD

DOLPHINS CAPTURE
THE HEARTS OF PEOPLE OF ALL AGES.

Not many can resist their playful nature and impressive intelligence. Even their appearance is charming. Dolphins' naturally upturned mouths give humans the impression that they're always smiling.

Two decades ago, the slaughter of dolphins by the tuna-fishing industry caused an uproar. People protested, boycotted tuna products, and wrote letters to their representatives. Congress passed laws that likely saved at-risk species from extinction. Due to dolphins' continued popularity, many countries established research and monitoring programs to ensure their survival.

These reforms have paid off. In 2009, biologists working in Bangladesh found a thriving population of 6,000 Irrawaddy dolphins. This species had been believed to be nearly extinct. Finds like these give experts hope that with protection and time even threatened dolphins can be saved.

Not all attempts to save dolphin species end in success. In 2006, scientists declared the Yangtze river dolphin, also called baiji, virtually extinct. The baiji became the first aquatic mammal to die out since hunting and overfishing killed off the Caribbean monk seal in the 1950s. For many scientists, it was a stinging loss. The baiji had been swimming the waters of the Yangtze River for 20 million years. Only in the last century have pollution, dams, overfishing, and propeller blades made their survival impossible.

Scientists and conservationists are determined to learn a lesson from the baiji, and not let

A bottlenose dolphin breaches the heavily polluted waters of Galveston Bay, Texas.

other species of dolphin meet the same fate. To accomplish this goal, scientists must understand all they can about dolphins. And there is much left to discover.

Scientists have many unanswered questions about dolphins. Much about their behavior, how they communicate, and how they forge social relationships is still not fully understood. Scientists don't know how global climate change is affecting many dolphin species. Or how dolphins respond to stress from pollution or natural disasters. Some dolphin scientists say that when one question is close to being answered, the answer itself causes more questions. Fortunately, that means that the fun you could have unraveling the mysteries of these amazing animals will last a lifetime.

HOW YOU CAN HELP
If you would like to help protect dolphins, visit http://www.defenders.org/wildlife_and_habitat/wildlife/dolphin.php for more information.

Irrawaddy dolphins live in harmony with Myanmar fishermen, who signal the dolphins to drive schools of fish into nets.

A pair of playful bottlenose dolphins splish and splash before going deep to grab dinner.

AN INTERACTIVE GLOSSARY

SWIM SMARTS

A bottlenose dolphin encounter at an aquarium culminates with a lift from a finned friend.

THESE WORDS ARE COMMONLY USED AMONG

DOLPHIN EXPERTS. Use the glossary to see what each word means. Then test your dolphin IQ. If you need help, visit the word's page numbers to see it used in context.

1. Adaptation
(PAGES 16–17)
An evolutionary change in an animal or plant that helps it live in a particular environment

Which adaptation best helps dolphins survive underwater?
a. chin hair
b. small ears
c. mammary glands
d. flippers and a fluke

2. Ancestor
(PAGES 12–13)
A related, earlier form of present-day animals

Which of the following is not true about the ancestors of modern dolphins?
a. They had legs.
b. They had hooves.
c. They walked on land.
d. They had scales.

3. Aquatic
(PAGES 18–19)
Living or growing in water

Which of the following animals is not aquatic?
a. squid
b. horse
c. orca
d. mackerel

4. Behavior
(PAGES 14–15, 36–37, 40–41)
The way in which living things act in response to their environment

Which behavior is common among male dolphins competing for a female?
a. They nudge each other to the surface.
b. They roll on their backs.
c. They snap their jaws aggressively.
d. They perform a front-flipping jump.

5. Baleen
(PAGES 12–13)

Baleen is a filtering structure that functions in place of ___ in some whales.
a. lungs
b. teeth
c. kidneys
d. nose hairs

6. Carnivore
(PAGES 28–29)
An animal that eats the flesh of other animals

What kind of teeth would you expect a carnivore to have?
a. sharp and pointy
b. square and flat
c. a mix of sharp and flat teeth
d. no teeth

7. Cetacean
(PAGES 12–13)
The group of marine mammals that includes porpoises, whales, and dolphins

Which of the following is not a cetacean?
a. sea lion
b. orca
c. bowhead whale
d. Risso's dolphin

8. Diet
(PAGES 28–29)
The foods eaten by a particular group of animals

Which organism can be part of an orca's diet?
a. shark
b. cow
c. plankton
d. seaweed

9. Echolocation
(PAGES 16–17, 18–19)
A system used by some animals for locating objects with sound waves

In which scenario would dolphins likely not use echolocation?
a. to find prey in murky water
b. to find prey hidden under sand
c. to find another member of the pod
d. to avoid obstacles in the dark

10. Habitat
(PAGES 14–15, 28–29)
The area in which an animal or plant normally lives

In which habitat are dolphins not likely to be found?
a. rivers
b. coastal areas
c. polar waters
d. desert watering holes

11. Mammal
(PAGES 6–7, 10–11, 12–13)
A warm-blooded animal whose young feed on milk that is produced by the mother

Which of the following is a feature of mammals?
a. cold-bloodedness
b. bodies covered in scales
c. high level of maternal care
d. meat-only diet

12. Pod
(PAGES 24–25, 42–43)
A group of dolphins

A dolphin pod is generally made up of ___.
a. newborns
b. males and females of all ages
c. related females
d. juvenile males

13. Population
(PAGES 38–39, 56–57)
A group of animals or plants of the same species that live in one place

Which dolphin population can often be found swimming with tuna?
a. southern Atlantic dolphins
b. eastern tropical Pacific dolphins
c. arctic dolphins
d. western Indian Ocean dolphins

14. Predator
(PAGES 18–19, 22–23)
An animal that hunts and eats other animals

Which of the following would a predator not eat?
a. algae
b. deer
c. squid
d. shrimp

15. Prey
(PAGES 28–29)
An animal that is hunted and eaten by another

Which of the following is typical prey for a bottlenose dolphin?
a. moose
b. mullet
c. shark
d. turtles

FIND OUT MORE

MOVIES TO WATCH

Dolphins: IMAX
Image Entertainment, 2004
Dolphins: Tribes of the Sea
Reel Productions LLC, 2006
20 Years With Dolphins
Digiview Entertainment, 2009

WEBSITES

Dolphin Research Center
www.dolphins.org

The Marine Mammal Center
www.tmmc.org

Ocean Conservation Society
www.oceanconservation.org

The Wild Dolphin Project
www.wilddolphinproject.org

BOOKS AND ARTICLES

Discovering Dolphins
Stephanie and Douglas Nowacek
Voyageur Press, 2006.
Face to Face With Dolphins
Flip and Linda Nicklin
National Geographic Children's Books, 2007.
Face to Face With Whales
Flip and Linda Nicklin
National Geographic Children's Books, 2008.
Meeting Dolphins: My Adventures in the Sea
Kathleen Dudzinski
National Geographic Society, 2000.
Oceans: Dolphins, Sharks, Penguins, and More!
Johnna Rizzo
National Geographic Children's Books, 2010.
"River Spirits"
Mark Jenkins, *National Geographic*. Washington, D.C.: June 2009.
"The Secret Language of Dolphins"
Crispin Boyer, *National Geographic Kids*. Washington, D.C.: June/July 2007.

PLACES TO VISIT

The most exciting way to learn about dolphins is to see them for yourself. Here are a few places where you can flip for dolphins!

Georgia Aquarium, Atlanta, Georgia
Mote Marine Aquarium, Sarasota, Florida
National Aquarium, Baltimore, Maryland
SeaWorld San Diego, San Diego, California
Shedd Aquarium, Chicago, Illinois

To the Bentley Girls —EC

Published by the National Geographic Society
John M. Fahey, Jr., *Chairman of the Board and Chief
Executive Officer*
Timothy T. Kelly, *President*
Declan Moore, *Executive Vice President; President,
Publishing*
Melina Gerosa Bellows, *Executive Vice President; Chief
Creative Officer, Books, Kids, and Family*

Prepared by the Book Division
Nancy Laties Feresten, *Senior Vice President, Editor in
Chief, Children's Books*
Jonathan Halling, *Design Director, Books and Children's
Publishing*
Jay Sumner, *Director of Photography, Children's
Publishing*
Jennifer Emmett, *Editorial Director, Children's Books*
Carl Mehler, *Director of Maps*
R. Gary Colbert, *Production Director*
Jennifer A. Thornton, *Managing Editor*

Staff for This Book
Priyanka Lamichhane, *Project Editor*
Eva Absher, *Art Director*
Lori Epstein, *Senior Illustrations Editor*
Annette Kiesow, *Illustrations Editor*
Simon Renwick, Erin Mayes, *Designers*
Grace Hill, *Associate Managing Editor*
Joan Gossett, *Production Editor*
Lewis R. Bassford, *Production Manager*
Susan Borke, *Legal and Business Affairs*
Kate Olesin, *Assistant Editor*
Kathryn Robbins, *Design Production Assistant*
Hillary Moloney, *Illustrations Assistant*

Manufacturing and Quality Management
Christopher A. Liedel, *Chief Financial Officer*
Phillip L. Schlosser, *Senior Vice President*
Chris Brown, *Technical Director*
Nicole Elliott, *Manager*
Rachel Faulise, *Manager*
Robert L. Barr, *Manager*

The National Geographic Society is one of
the world's largest nonprofit scientific and
educational organizations. Founded in
1888 to "increase and diffuse geographic
knowledge," the Society works to inspire
people to care about the planet. National
Geographic reflects the world through its magazines,
television programs, films, music and radio, books, DVDs,
maps, exhibitions, live events, school publishing
programs, interactive media and merchandise. *National
Geographic* magazine, the Society's official journal,
published in English and 33 local-language editions, is
read by more than 38 million people each month. The
National Geographic Channel reaches 320 million
households in 34 languages in 166 countries. National
Geographic Digital Media receives more than 15 million
visitors a month. National Geographic has funded more
than 9,400 scientific research, conservation and
exploration projects and supports an education program
promoting geography literacy. For more information, visit
nationalgeographic.com.

For more information, please call 1-800-NGS LINE
(647-5463) or write to the following address:
National Geographic Society
1145 17th Street N.W.
Washington, DC 20036-4688 U.S.A.

Visit us online at www.nationalgeographic.com/books

For librarians and teachers: www.ngchildrensbooks.org

More for kids from National Geographic:
kids.nationalgeographic.com

For information about special discounts for bulk
purchases, please contact National Geographic Books
Special Sales: ngspecsales@ngs.org

For rights or permissions inquiries, please contact
National Geographic Books Subsidiary Rights:
ngbookrights@ngs.org

Library of Congress Cataloging-in-Publication Data
Carney, Elizabeth, 1981-
National Geographic Kids everything dolphins : all the
dolphin facts, photos, and fun that will make you flip / by
Elizabeth Carney.—1st ed.
    p. cm.
Includes bibliographical references and index.
ISBN 978-1-4263-0842-0 (pbk. : alk. paper)—
ISBN 978-1-4263-0843-7 (library binding : alk. paper)
1. Dolphins—Juvenile literature. I. National Geographic
Society (U.S.) II. Title.
QL737.C432C28 2012
599.53—dc23
                                2011025753

Printed in China
11/TS/1